Christmas

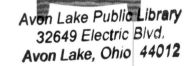

BY TRUDI STRAIN TRUEIT • ILLUSTRATED BY JAN BRYAN-HUNT

The Child's World®

Published by The Child's World®
1980 Lookout Drive • Mankato, MN 56003-1705
800-599-READ • www.childsworld.com

Acknowledgments
The Child's World®: Mary Berendes, Publishing Director
The Design Lab: Design
Jody Jensen Shaffer: Editing

ISBN 9781623235147
LCCN 2013931399

Printed in the United States of America
Mankato, MN
July, 2013
PA02169

ABOUT THE AUTHOR

Trudi Strain Trueit is a former television
news reporter and anchor. She has
written more than forty books for
children. She lives in Everett, WA with
her husband, Bill, a teacher.

ABOUT THE ILLUSTRATOR

Jan Bryan-Hunt is a freelance illustrator
living with her husband and two
children in the Kansas City area.

Table of Contents

The star is an important Christmas **symbol**. Christians believe that long ago three wise men were guided by a star to Bethlehem to give gifts to the newborn baby Jesus. Today, in places like Russia, Italy, and Poland, the holiday officially begins when the first star appears in the sky on Christmas Eve.

CHAPTER 1

Christmas Is Here!

Colored lights and shiny **ornaments** make a fir tree sparkle. See how the gold star at the top glows? Brightly wrapped gifts are piled beneath the tree. Everything is ready for Christmas!

Christmas is a joyful holiday. For Christians, it is a day to celebrate the birth of Jesus Christ. The word Christmas means "the Mass of Christ" or the "festival of Christ."

Family and friends gather on this holiday to eat and exchange gifts. It is a time to show those you love how much you care about them. So smile and say, "Merry Christmas!"

Trees and stars are often seen at Christmastime.

CHAPTER 2

Tree of Light and Beauty

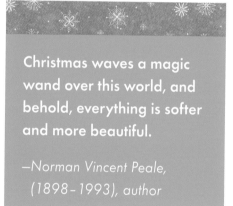

Christmas waves a magic wand over this world, and behold, everything is softer and more beautiful.

—Norman Vincent Peale, (1898-1993), author

People began celebrating Christmas about 1,700 years ago. The Christian book of worship, the Bible, does not give the exact date that Christ was born. Early Christians chose to celebrate the holiday on December 25th.

Originally, Christmas was called the Feast of the Nativity. Nativity means "birth." It was a public festival where people came to eat, sing, and dance. In time, people began celebrating the holiday with their families.

There are many legends about the first Christmas tree. One story says that in 1510 a German preacher

*The **tradition** of decorating Christmas trees began over 500 years ago!*

named Martin Luther was strolling through the forest on Christmas Eve. The snow-covered trees were so lovely that Martin cut one to take home. He decorated the tree with candles. These were the first Christmas lights!

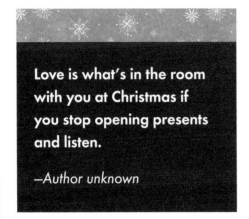

Giving a gift is one of many Christmas customs.

CHAPTER 3

Gifts of the Season

Christians believe the first Christmas gifts were gold, **frankincense**, and **myrrh**. These were given to the baby Jesus by the three wise men.

About 700 years ago, people in Europe began exchanging Christmas presents. By the 1700s,

the custom spread to North America. Originally, children got small gifts, like candy or fruit.

In the United States, children eagerly await the arrival of Santa Claus on Christmas Eve. Santa leaves toys and treats in stockings hung by the fireplace. In Germany, the jolly fellow is known as Saint Nicholas. In Russia, he is called Father Frost.

In the 1840s, English illustrator John Callcott Horsley drew one of the first commercial Christmas cards. It showed a family sharing Christmas dinner. Today, people in the United States send more than two billion Christmas cards each year!

Christmas gift suggestions:
To your enemy, forgiveness.
To an opponent, tolerance.
To a friend, your heart.
To a customer, service.
To all, charity.
To every child,
a good example.
To yourself, respect.

—Oren Arnold (1900–1980)

Many people send Christmas cards every year.

During Christmas, many families display a nativity. The scene shows baby Jesus in a manger. Mary, Joseph, the three wise men, shepherds, animals, and angels are also part of the nativity.

For many families, a nativity scene is an important Christmas decoration.

CHAPTER 4

Deck the Halls

Can you imagine Christmas without decorations? From tiny sprigs of mistletoe to giant **inflatable** snow globes, decorations are a big part of the holiday season.

Some Christians set up a nativity scene in their home to honor the birth of Christ. Other families display an Advent wreath. The wreath has four candles and lays flat on a table. Each week in December, one candle on the wreath is lit until all four are burning during Christmas week.

It's great fun to decorate a Christmas tree. Strings of lights, tinsel garlands, and ornaments make the tree glitter. Does your family put up a Christmas tree? How do you like to decorate it?

Mexican children celebrate Christmas with a piñata, which is a papier-mâché animal filled with candy, coins, and gifts. Each child is blindfolded before trying to break open the piñata with a stick.

Christmas dinner is a time for families to gather.

CHAPTER 5

Food and Fun

Christmas wouldn't be the same without cookies, fudge, and other goodies. In North America, many families have a large Christmas dinner. They eat turkey, mashed potatoes, and cranberry sauce. In Norway, preserved codfish called lutefisk (LOO-tuh-fisk) is a popular Christmas dish. People in Great Britain often serve goose or turkey with potatoes and

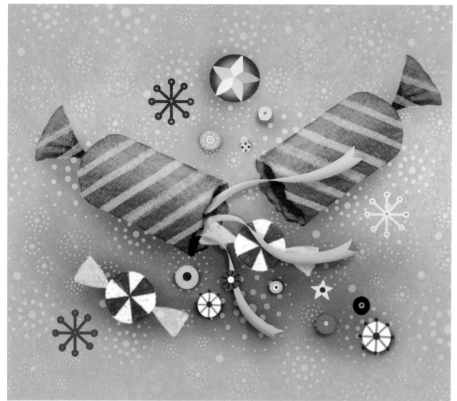

Crackers are filled with candy and small toys.

Christmas pudding. Sometimes, the pudding holds coins or charms for children.

British children also like crackers. These crackers are not a food. A cracker is a colorful paper tube that is twisted at both ends. When the twists are pulled, the cracker goes *pop!* and small toys fall out of the tube.

Our hearts grow tender with childhood memories and love of kindred, and we are better throughout the year for having, in spirit, become a child again at Christmas-time.

—Laura Ingalls Wilder (1867–1957)

> I will honor Christmas in my heart, and try to keep it all the year.
>
> —Charles Dickens (1812 - 1870)

Family and friends sing Christmas carols at Christmastime.

CHAPTER 6

Peace on Earth

Many Christians around the world go to church on Christmas Eve. They may listen to religious leaders read the story of Christ's birth. The **sermon** reminds them to be kind and giving to others. Some churches

hold a special candlelight service at midnight. It is magical to see so many candles flickering as people sing *Silent Night*.

Each family who celebrates Christmas has its own traditions. Some people like to visit friends on Christmas Eve, sing **carols**, or make cookies to leave for Santa. Does your family have any special holiday traditions?

Some families open their presents on Christmas Eve, while others prefer to unwrap them on Christmas morning. Either way, it can be so hard to wait to see what's inside all those wonderful packages!

Leave some milk and cookies for Santa!

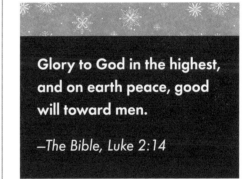

Glory to God in the highest, and on earth peace, good will toward men.

—The Bible, Luke 2:14

CHAPTER 7

Poetry Corner

CHRISTMAS BELLS

I heard the bells on Christmas Day

Their old, familiar carols play,

And wild and sweet

The words repeat

Of peace on earth, good-will to men!

—*Henry Wadsworth Longfellow (1807–1882)*

MISTLETOE

Sitting under the mistletoe
(Pale-green, fairy mistletoe),
One last candle burning low,
All the sleepy dancers gone,
Just one candle burning on,
Shadows lurking everywhere:
Some one came, and kissed me there.

—*Walter de la Mare (1873–1956)*

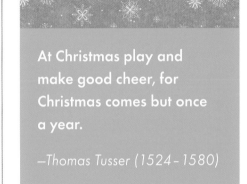

At Christmas play and make good cheer, for Christmas comes but once a year.

—*Thomas Tusser (1524–1580)*

THE NIGHT BEFORE CHRISTMAS
(A Visit from Saint Nicholas)

'Twas the night before Christmas,
When all through the house
Not a creature was stirring, not even a mouse.
The stockings were hung by the chimney with care,
In hopes that St. Nicholas soon would be there.

The children were nestled all snug in their beds,
While visions of sugar-plums danced in their heads.
And mamma in her 'kerchief, and I in my cap,
Had just settled our brains for a long winter's nap.

When out on the lawn there arose such a clatter,
I sprang from the bed to see what was the matter.
Away to the window I flew like a flash,
Tore open the shutters and threw up the sash.

The moon on the breast of the new-fallen snow

Gave the lustre of mid-day to objects below.

When, what to my wondering eyes should appear,

But a miniature sleigh, and eight tiny reindeer.

—*Selection by Clement Clarke Moore (1779–1863)*

CHAPTER 8

Songs of Christmas

JOY TO THE WORLD

Joy to the world, the Lord is come!

Let earth receive her King;

Let every heart prepare Him room,

And Heaven and nature sing,

And Heaven and nature sing,

And Heaven, and Heaven, and nature sing.

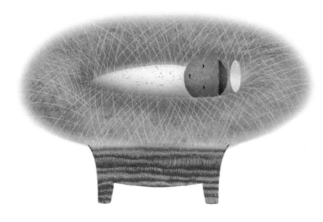

SILENT NIGHT

Silent night! Holy night!
All is calm, all is bright;
Round yon Virgin Mother and Child!
Holy Infant, so tender and mild,
Sleep in heavenly peace,
Sleep in heavenly peace.

Silent night! Holy night!
Shepherds quake at the sight!
Glories stream from Heaven afar,
Heavenly Hosts sing Alleluia!
Christ, the Savior, is born,
Christ, the Savior, is born!

—*words by Josef Mohr (1792–1848),*
translated by John F. Young (1820–1885)

JINGLE BELLS

Dashing through the snow in a one-horse open sleigh,
O'er the fields we go laughing all the way.
Bells on bob tails ring, making spirits bright,
What fun it is to laugh and sing a sleighing song tonight.

Oh, jingle bells, jingle bells, jingle all the way.
Oh, what fun it is to ride in a one-horse open sleigh.
Jingle bells, jingle bells, jingle all the way.
Oh, what fun it is to ride in a one-horse open sleigh.

WE WISH YOU A MERRY CHRISTMAS

We wish you a Merry Christmas;
We wish you a Merry Christmas;
We wish you a Merry Christmas and a Happy New Year.
Good tidings we bring to you and your kin;
Good tidings for Christmas and a Happy New Year.

Joining in the Spirit of Christmas

* Peace, love, and goodwill are major themes of Christmas. Think of some ways you can reach out to others during the holiday season. It might be as easy as giving away clothes that no longer fit or helping a parent clean the house.

* Do you know someone from another country? Ask how to say "Merry Christmas" in his or her native language and learn how your friend celebrates Christmas.

* Does your family have a special holiday tradition? Perhaps you make a gingerbread house or wrap presents for those in need. How important is it for you to keep those traditions alive when you grow up and have children of your own?

* Make home made Christmas cookies, cards, or ornaments. Give them to those who have done something nice for you this year, like your coach or a teacher.

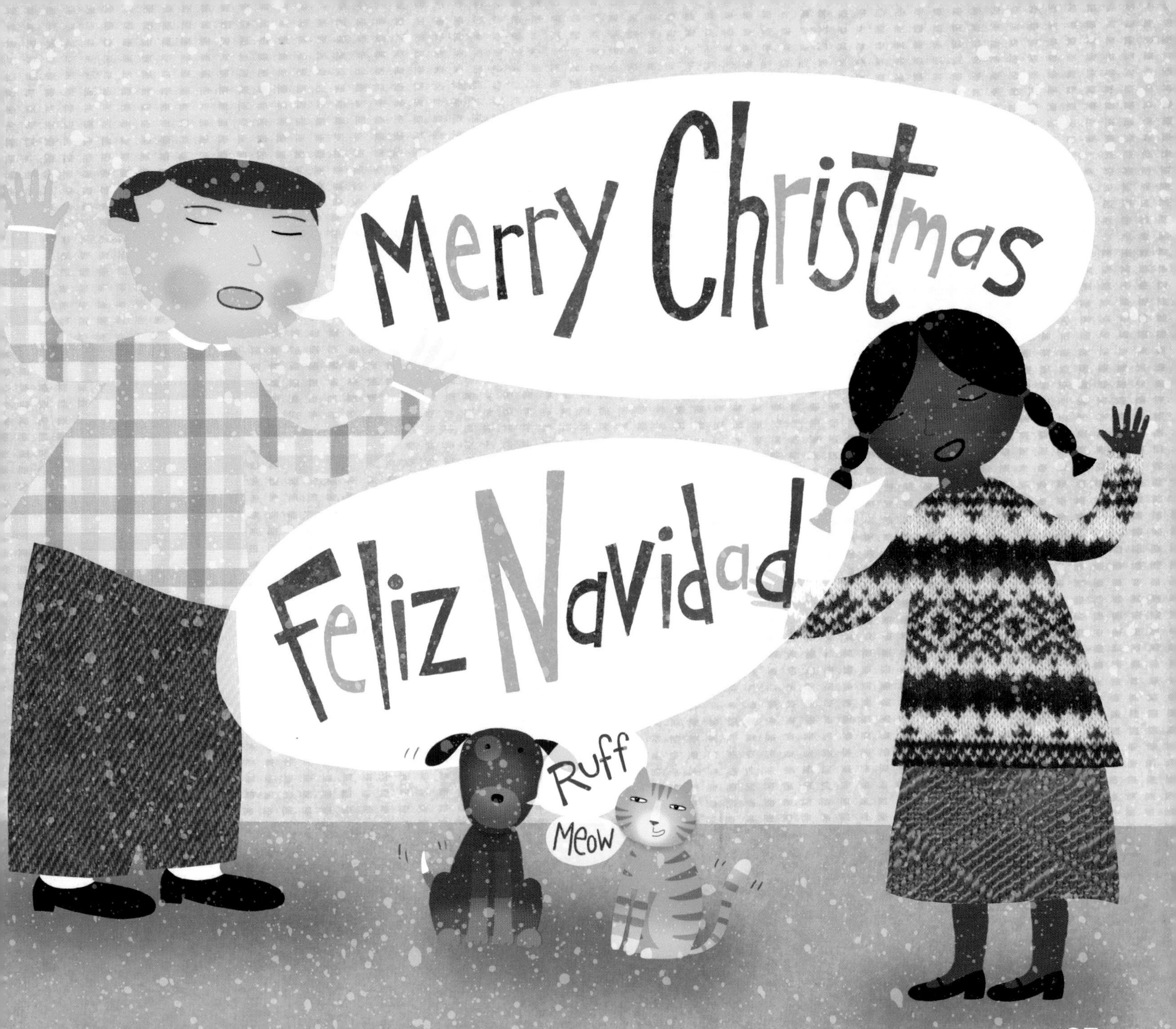
Merry Christmas
Feliz Navidad
Ruff
Meow

Build a Gingerbread House

What you need:

8-10 graham crackers
Empty milk carton
(school size)
Styrofoam meat tray (washed)
Colorful hard candies
   (peppermint, gumdrops, sprinkles, etc.)
Tube frosting with different tips
White frosting

Directions

1. Place the milk carton on the Styrofoam tray. Spread the white frosting on the outside of the milk carton.
2. Use the frosting to "glue" four graham crackers on the outside of the milk carton. These will be the walls.
3. With the frosting, glue one graham cracker on top of your gingerbread house. This will be the base of the roof.
4. To make a pointed roof, lean two graham crackers on the roof's base. Secure them with more frosting.
5. Decorate the house. The white frosting looks like snow, so it's fun to spread some on the roof and around the outside of the house. Use the tube frosting to make fancy trim, windows, or doorways. Use small candies for trimmings and decoration.

Making Reindeer Cookies

What you need:

1 cup brown sugar

1 cup sugar

1 cup butter, softened

1 cup smooth peanut butter

2 eggs

$^1/_2$ teaspoon salt

1 teaspoon vanilla

3 cups flour (scant)

2 teaspoons baking soda

Small pretzel sticks and
red and green candy pieces

Mixer

Large bowl

Measuring spoons

Measuring cups

Directions

1. Cream the butter and sugars, eggs and peanut butter, salt and vanilla.
2. Add the soda and flour and mix well.
3. Roll into balls (about the size of a golf ball).
4. Flatten the ball and shape it into a triangle.
5. Place pretzel pieces into 2 of the triangle corners for antlers.
6. Place a red candy at the other corner (Rudolph's red nose), and 2 green candies on the cookie for eyes.
7. Bake at 375 degrees* for 10-12 minutes or until golden brown.

When the cookies are done, share them with someone in the spirit of Christmas!

Have an adult help you operate the oven.

Glossary

carols—joyful Christmas songs or hymns

frankincense—a perfume that is burned for religious ceremonies

inflatable—an object that can have air blown or pumped into it

myrrh—a strong perfume from trees

ornaments—beautiful decorations

sermon—a religious message meant to teach a lesson

symbol—an object that stands for an idea

tradition—a long-held custom or something people do every year

Learn More

Books

Bull, Jane. *The Merry Christmas Activity Book*. New York: Dorling Kindersley, 2005.

Ingalls, Ann. *Christmas Traditions around the World*. Mankato, MN: The Child's World, 2013.

Moore, Clement Clarke. *The Night Before Christmas*. New York: HarperCollins, 2006.

Sadler, Judy Anne. *Christmas Crafts from Around the World*. Tonawanda, NY: Kids Can Press, 2003.

Web Sites

Visit our Web site for links about Christmas and other holidays:

childsworld.com/links

Note to Parents, Teachers, and Librarians: We routinely verify our Web links to make sure they are safe and active sites. So encourage your readers to check them out!

Index

11/13